Jehovah Jireh
(OUR PROVIDER)

"Thou openest thine hand, and satisfiest the desire of every living thing. The LORD is righteous in all his ways, and holy in all his works." Psalm 145:16-17

ESTHER MARIE ZIPH

WestBow Press books may be ordered through booksellers or by contacting:

WestBow Press
A Division of Thomas Nelson & Zondervan
1663 Liberty Drive
Bloomington, IN 47403
www.westbowpress.com
844-714-3454

Interior Image Credit: Esther Marie Ziph

Scripture taken from the King James Version of the Bible.

ISBN: 978-1-6642-6479-3 (sc)
ISBN: 978-1-6642-6481-6 (hc)
ISBN: 978-1-6642-6480-9 (e)

Library of Congress Control Number: 2022907745

Print information available on the last page.

WestBow Press rev. date: 05/21/2022

WESTBOW
PRESS®
A DIVISION OF THOMAS NELSON
& ZONDERVAN

Dedicated to...

My Lord and Savior Jesus Christ

&

My parents who loved me like Jesus

Lord, I worship Your Name
Yours alone
There is none I'd rather
Jesus Lord
I bow before Your throne
In awe.
Love AK

"In the beginning God created the heaven and the earth." Gen 1:1

"Through faith we understand that the worlds were framed by the word of God, so that things which are seen were not made of things which do appear." Hebrews 11:3

Lord, thank you for the knowledge that You are the Creator and Sustainer of all life in this world. Thank you for creating us in such perfection that if one nucleotide in a replicating DNA strand malfunctions we pass on at conception [1]. Thank You for the program of life we have found exists in every one of our 100 trillion cells [1]. Our hearts stand amazed at the care you have for each of us as we grow from a single cell to a full-grown adult. All our effort and knowledge could never create a single cell never mind breathe it into effect. What God is it that would spend His time designing the laws of thermodynamics, gravity, and physics to protect and surround such ungrateful creatures such as us? Lord, we are a masterpiece! An infinitely complex and delicate balance of water and dust. I am humbled by Your love and design.

Love, AK

As the deer panteth for the water
So my soul longeth after Thee.
You alone are my heart's desire
And I long to worship Thee.

You alone are my strength, my shield
To You alone may my spirit yield.
You alone are my heart's desire
And I long to worship Thee.

(lyric by Martin Nystrom 1981) 3

"And the earth was without form, and void; and darkness was upon the face of the deep. And the Spirit of God moved upon the face of the waters." Genesis 1:2

"Neither is there salvation in any other: for there is none other name under heaven given among men, whereby we must be saved." Acts 4:12

Lord, our hearts and lives are so void of purpose, form and thus joy without You. Nothing in this world makes sense without You in the equation. Where do we come from? Where is the beginning and the ending of the universe around us? What can fill our heart and satisfy? Lord, move upon the Water of Your Word. May the words of Truth overflow each heart who reads them. May You dispel the darkness of lying, jealousy, and guilt that weasel their way into holes in our hearts. May we fill those holes, those empty desires with You. We need Your salvation more than anything else this world has to offer. Please save us from the physical and emotional damage that comes as a result of lack of trust in Your goodness. Please flood our hearts with Your Word. We need you Lord! As individuals, as a nation and as a world. Only You can form us into the Christ-like people we need to be. May we be willing and anxious to put our focus heavenward. We are mere dust, but when dust goes heavenward and mixes with water (The Word of God); refreshment of rain pours down to earth for the next generation of life and nourishes it. Lord, may Your Word transform us into a refreshing rain of Your Spirit for others to absorb and grow thereby.

Your Words make my feet want to soar
Bring hope, healing, forgiveness
and more.
Thank you for Your Word complete and holy.
Said to the lost, destitute and
lowly.
Who are we? Blasphemers of Your Name.
To receive such grace? We are glad You came.
For what hope have we to be free from sin?
It's chains dark & we don't know we are in.
Please save us now and forever more.
Please teach us to be free and learn to soar.
Love, AK

"And God said, Let there be light: and there was light." Genesis 1:3

"But blessed are your eyes, for they see: and your ears, for they hear." Matthew 13:16

Lord, only You can speak light into this world we call home. Light travels at 186,000 miles per second in all directions$_2$ and yet only the creation You have put on this earth can see it. You have created light for so many amazing purposes. Light illuminates and dispels darkness giving us the ability to see our surroundings and what direction we are going. Light bounces off objects scattering some wavelengths and absorbing others to reveal a beautiful tapestry of colors and patterns woven into this universe. Light is in essence a part of Your being and thus should be a part of ours. May we use each morning, afternoon, and evening light to absorb and praise the gifts of light that You have given us. Please cause the light of the Word of God to enter our hearts and reveal the darkness of sin inside. Sin corrodes the heart, mind and body. Without Your guiding light to reveal sin we degrade to nothing but dirt and a black burning hole called Hades. May we accept Your Word Lord and like a candle the brightness of it cheer, lead, and help all those around us. We only have a few hours here on earth, but Lord teach us how to shine the goodness You have given in Word and deed.

Change my heart, O God,
Make it ever true.
Change my heart, O God,
May I be like You.
You are the Potter
I am the clay
Mold me and make me
This is what I pray.
(lyric by Eddie Espinosa 1982) [3]

"There is a candle in every soul
Some brightly burning, some dark and cold
There is a Spirit who brings the fire
Ignites a candle and makes His home

Refrain
So carry your candle, run to the darkness
Seek out the helpless, confused and torn
Hold out your candle for all to see it
Take your candle, and go light your world."
(lyric by Chris Rice) [20]

"And God saw the light, that it was good: and God divided the light from the darkness." Genesis 1:4

"Then spake Jesus again unto them, saying, I am the light of the world: he that followeth me shall not walk in darkness, but shall have the light of life." John 8:12

"Let your light so shine before men, that they may see your good works, and glorify Your Father which is in heaven." Matthew 5:16

Lord Jesus, thank you for giving up Your Godhead to be a light for poor wretched sinners such as us. We are helplessly prone to every iniquity and unable to do otherwise without Your saving blood. May our hearts be full of Your light so there are no shadows in our hearts and closed doors. Magnify your Word in us and multiply our thoughts of You. Show us the full spectrum of Your love and may we be still in spirit enough to reflect it. Sharing the attributes of Your Greatness means forgetting ourselves and focusing on the eternal. May we have the courage to never give up the light no matter how dark of a place You have placed us in. You are the light of the world and the closer we draw to You the farther the darkness will retreat. Thank you for the peace, security, and confidence that accompany walking near the Creator of the Universe. Lord, we lie prostrate in the knowledge that You are the only one true light and hope for this world. May we overflow with adoration for your perfect plan. And when the world or circumstances try to break us; may the ones around us be overcome by the full spectrum of Christ-like attributes that meet their eyes. "Shew me thy ways, O Lord; teach me thy paths. Lead me in thy truth, and teach me for thou art the God of my Salvation; on thee do I wait all the day." Psalm 25:4-5

Behold, He calls us nearer
We run to His arms
There is none dearer
Forever is His Love
We will never get enough
His life He gave for us
Amazing love!
Now we are free.
Such passions we have never known
Go far beyond our dreams
Our love for Him has grown
Only Him we see.
His grace, goodness, love
We want always to pass on
Unmatched and true from above
May it radiate like the Sun.
Who is the One who opens my heart
Fills it with love and does not depart?
Who is the One who shattered my sin
Set me free with joy and peace again.
Who is the one who calls my name
Over and over until I respond in same?
Who is the One who rules by day
By night, by hour and never far away?
Who is the One I can't live without
His tender words I shouldn't doubt?
Who is the One abandoned by all
Yet forgave? I answer His call.

For only God could have hung on that tree
Abandoned for you and for me!
Why? Why? Would He?
He created us and knows our frame
He knew sin dominated and we would be the same
Unless! Unless! He turned the tide
Modeled righteousness and sin did hide.
For only God had strength to do
The sacrifice He did for you.
A proof of His dedication and love
No matter the circumstances on earth and above.
Amen! Amen! The song rings out
He saved us! We will all shout
For only God could have hung on that tree
And brought life, love, and liberty!
Thank You Lord!

It aint over until God says its' over.

"And God called the light Day, and the darkness he called Night, And the evening and the morning were the first day." Genesis 1:5

"Ye are all the children of light, and the children of day: we are not of the night, nor of darkness. Therefore let us not sleep, as do others; but let us watch and be sober. For they that sleep sleep in the night; and they that be drunken are drunken in the night. But let us, who are of the day, be sober, putting on the breastplate of faith and love; and for an helmet, the hope of salvation. For God hath not appointed us to wrath, but to obtain salvation by our Lord Jesus Christ, Who died for us, that, whether we wake or sleep, we should live together with him." I Thessalonians 5: 5-10

Lord, thank you for the day You confronted each of us with the issue of our sins, and offered a remedy to forever cleanse us of its deadly stronghold on our hearts and lives.

Don't give up! Don't give in!
The devil wants to win!
Don't give up! Lift Your eyes!
Above the clouds arise!
Don't give up! He is here!
In prayer draw near!
Don't give up! Winds assail!
It makes you want to bail!
Don't give up! The Lord reigns!
He erases all the stains!
Don't give up! Shout for joy!
He calls you to deploy!
Don't give up! Don't give in!
The devil wants to win!

We know Lord that we will have those seasons of light, joy and happiness as well as those seasons of darkness, grief and pain. All we ask is that You will walk with us in each day that You bring. Draw us nearer to Your side and give us an overwhelming desire to please you in all things. We are the delicate work of Your Hand now granted new abundant life in Christ. Teach us how to share the abundant promises You have given each one of us with our family, friends, neighbors, authorities, and even our enemies.

God,

I lay myself bare and naked before You like these winter trees. Throwing my hands, my fingers upward in desperate need of Your light. I accept Your light into my innermost being and I know that you will convert Your light into the Fruits of the Spirit in me. My fruits are gone this season, whithered, cast away and consumed by greedy men. I pray for the warmth of spring to once again coax the buds of hope, and virtue, forgiveness, and love once again out of me. The leaves of prosperity, youth and vigor are gone. Composted all around me turning into fertile soil for the next generation in my neighbor's family, and friends. My form is laid bare, exposed for all to see against a grey sky of untruths floating towards me. A few shreds of last year's dreams hang to my branches like ragged and dried tissues. I have many scars where the fruit of my body has been plucked.

There is a peace in this season though. All the strivings have ceased. There are no facades of pretty leaf wrappings or blossoms constantly blooming to consider pollinating. The busy bees are not constantly scoping you out for more of your sweet nectar. The busy squirrels and birds are not making another nest in your "hair." I am at peace in this season. All the scars are exposed and the structure and strength of my character are on display for all to see. I am not ashamed. There is a stillness, a contentment with being totally myself with arms upraised to an Almighty God, and not be able to "do" anything else. There is nothing to hide from God and man and there is nothing to fear.

The same God who has built me and formed me into the testimony of His Grace is the same God who grants me every breath, word, and thought. How could I fear a God who has built billions of neuron transfers just inside my small brain that work together perfectly to allow me to write this? How could I be ashamed of the DNA structure He planned uniquely just for me to become? How could I bemoan the path because the roses have thorns and the mosquitos are a valuable food source for birds? How can I give anything but awe to the Creator of all things who doeth all things well?

So all this winter season long, I am committed to, like the trees, raise my hands in worship no matter the weather. Waiting, expectantly and consistently for the light of God to fall and warm me with His Presence. That I too may have the buds of hope, joy, and bubbling laughter and fruits of righteousness, compassion, and love from now until the day I die and go be with my Maker.

Today is Your day and yours alone
For us to praise and worship Your Name
You sacrificed all for our vile sins
Lord Jesus we are thankful that you came

The agony You bore can't compare
To any suffering we may face
You are our all-compassionate friend
Faithful as we run the Christian race

Lord Jesus Christ you died for our sins
No other name above is so dear
For Your amazing atoning love
Grips our hearts in awe and holy fear

Savior Jesus hold us close to You
To You we release our burdened life
What wondrous freedom we do see
For focusing on Him removes strife

Humbly our Savior walked this earth
Jesus please mold us to reflect You
In grace, goodness, mercy, truth and love
In everything we think, say and do.

"And God said, Let there be a firmament (Heb. expanse) in the midst of the waters, and let it divide the waters from the waters." Genesis 1:6

"But when they came to Jesus, and saw that he was dead already, they brake not his legs: But one of the soldiers with a spear pierced his side, and forthwith came there out blood and water." John 19:33-34

Lord, how amazed we are at Your perfect plan instituted and reiterated to us over and over again in Your Word. You created this world with such detail. Giving us land to live on amidst a wonderful world of water. Just as if we were to try and drink the oceans dry we could never ingest the full spectrum of Your love for us. You keep us physically safe on land and feed our physical thirst with water; but You keep us spiritually saved on the Rock of Jesus and feed our spiritual thirst with The Word of God the living water. Only God Almighty would allow the separation of blood and water in His Son's body to save us from the inevitable flood of sin in our lives. Every day our actions and thoughts spear Your loving heart Lord and we beg for Your forgiveness. We don't deserve any of the loving gifts You have given us and we could never write even a fraction of them for they are so numerous. Thank you for separating the truths of scripture (our spiritual water) so we could see clearly the plan of saving grace You instituted from the beginning to rescue our dying souls. Love, AK

The person of Christ,
Enfolding every grace,
Once slain, but now alive again,
In heaven demands our praise.

Gladly of Him we sing,
Since we with Him are dead:
Our life is hid with Christ in God,
In Christ the church's Head.

The heavens are opened now!
Sound it through the earth abroad;
And we, by faith, in HEAVEN behold
Jesus the Christ, our Lord.

-G.V. Wigram

Omnipotent, Holy Lamb of God
Why did You die for me?
I'm a sinner, not deserving Your love
From Your Face I did flee.

Over and Over You called my name
I listened but did not reply.
My life was totally clogged with sin
You washed it away with a cry.

Eli, Eli Lama Sabachthani
You took my place on the tree.
Why did you give me such a beautiful gift
To go to heaven for free?

Face to Face, I met you my Lord
Trembling, I begged for mercy.
You gently leaned down to pick me up
Your loving embrace engulfed me.

Crying, I stayed safely in Your arms
Your power gave me strength.
Omnipotent, Holy Lamb of God
Your love, for me, knows no length.

"And God made the firmament, and divided the waters which were under the firmament from the waters which were above the firmament: and it was so." Genesis 1:7

"Study to shew thyself approved unto God, a workman that needeth not to be ashamed, rightly dividing the word of truth." II Timothy 2:15

Lord, thank you for dividing and clarifying right and wrong, sin and righteousness, gold and chaff, earthly and heavenly, vain words and eternal words. So many of our spoken words have no meaning and no validity to them compared to the refreshing water of Your Word. May our hearts and minds be trained to output Your words of truth and love. May we not be ashamed of the standard and accompanying graces You have established for this world. We are Your workmanship and only here for a blink of time. "For we brought nothing into this world, and it is certain we can carry nothing out." 1 Timothy 6:7 May You teach us to have words that flow forth and water the souls of ones around us. May our words not be like a light dew that gives only temporary relief from the heat of the day, but as a strong rain that penetrates the roots of the ones we meet and promotes spiritual growth. Our mouths and hearts are Yours Lord, for only You can rightly divide the Word of Truth which is the Water of Life to our souls.

Give of your best to the Master;
Give of the strength of your youth;
Throw your souls fresh, glowing ardor
Into the battle for truth.
Jesus has set the example,
Dauntless was He, young and brave;
Give Him your loyal devotion;
Give Him the best that you have.

Give of your best to the Master;
Give Him first place in your heart;
Give Him first place in your service;
Consecrate every part.
Give, and to you will be given;
God His beloved Son gave;
Gratefully seeking to serve Him,
Give Him the best that you have.
(lyric Howard Grose) 3

The Journey

Lord we trust You for all
      Thanks for peace and comfort in prayer.
Yes, we do often fall
      Your grace, mercy, and love are rare.
The true calm in the storm
      Comes with prayer and His listening ear.
While character will form
      He wants our best, and we have no fear.
      Glory to our Lord God
Whom all the skies and seas obey.
      His will we often trod
As we listen may we seek His way.

God's walking on the blue sky-roads today:
  See, how lovely the dust of His feet.
  "Clouds of dust", we say down here
As it whirls through our troubled atmosphere
And we walk in the thick of it; but up there,
"The clouds are the dust of His feet," they say.
      By Amy Carmichael) [17]

**"And God called the firmament Heaven. And the evening and the morning were the second day."
Genesis 1:8**

"The heavens declare the glory of God; and the firmament sheweth his handywork. Day unto day uttereth speech, and night unto night sheweth knowledge. There is no speech nor language, where their voice is not heard. Their line is gone out through all the earth, and their words to the end of the world. In them hath he set a tabernacle for the sun, which is as a bridegroom coming out of his chamber, and rejoiceth as a strong man to run a race. His going forth is from the end of heaven, and his circuit unto the ends of it: and there is nothing hid from the heat thereof." Psalm 19:1-6

Lord, thank You for creating the world to be surrounded with such beauty in our sky. You promise each saved one a place in Heaven and it must be overwhelmingly spectacular if it is better than what You have made for us here. The beauty NASA shows us of all Your incredible designs is overwhelming. Thank You for not making the earth the center of the universe, but giving us a realistic picture of what our position is in creation. Our earth is tucked in a far corner of the the Milky Way Galaxy [4]. We are Your worshippers and we stand in awe of the power You display in stars, nebulas, galaxies, vortexes, black holes and planets. Everything You have made is moving and planets and neutrons, stars and electrons alike are orbiting [4] because of Your force, Your Power. You Lord, hold all of this together and how dare we think anything of ourselves in the light of Your Glory.

Our Lord, our fulfillment
of everything
Our Lord, our boundless joy
To Him we sing.
Our Lord, our Creator
All knowing King.
Our Lord, His endless love
To us He will bring

Grasping our hearts with joyful worship
The golden rays are burned in our eyes forever
We are in awe......
Hues of His Glory adorn each cloud in majesty
Glowing more golden with each passing moment
Walks on the tips of the clouds
Our Lord.

"And God said, Let the waters under the heaven be gathered together unto one place, and let the dry land appear: and it was so." Genesis 1:9

"…that also he should gather together in one the children of God that were scattered abroad." John 11:52

"For where two or three are gathered together in my name, there am I in the midst of them." Matthew 18:20

Lord, we know that Your plan is to gather your children who are full of Your living water into one place called Heaven. Our existence is only to praise and adore You in this life and for eternity. May the truth of Your Word unite the ones who have confessed with their mouth that Jesus is Lord. We are a scattered people in spirit, soul and body. May the reading of Your Word be a real and vigorous exercise that makes each one see clearly the path You have laid before them. You don't want us swimming and overwhelmed by the Holy Bible, but have a firm grasp of all You have revealed to us. This way we can walk on the solid and unwavering Truth that Jesus, Holy Jesus died for our sins. He is the absolute atonement for a human race proven to be incapable of heavenly perfection. Lord, we know that each of us are made in Your image, and made to shine forth Your Glory. Bring us together on the solid Word of God as a nation and as a world. May we be like the refrain …

"Standing, Standing,
standing on the promises of God my Savior;
Standing, standing,
I'm standing on the promises of God.
(lyric by R. Kelso Carter 1886) ₃

26

Lord, I have a burden
My friends and family argue
They look at each other
With hate and jealousy
Why Lord?
It tears your heart more than mine!
Why Lord?
Can any good come of this?
Yes, You are I AM
And I realize You know what is best
You promised that everything
Is in Your Hands.
Is there anything I can do?

"Pray without ceasing."
1 Thessalonians 5:17
Is there anything I can say?
"Speak the truth in love."
Ephesians 4:15
Is there anywhere I can go?
"Walk in love."
Ephesians 5:2
My life is in Your hands
May the emotions and storms of the moment
Clear the way to a deeper love of You
And unite our hearts
In the body of Christ
For You are the great I AM.

I'm so glad You came to save us.
You came from heaven to earth
To show the way
From the earth to the cross
My debt to pay
From the cross to the grave
From the grave to the sky
Lord, I lift Your name on high.
(lyric by Rick Founds) 21

"And God called the dry land Earth; and the gathering together of the waters called he Seas: and God saw that it was good." Genesis 1:10

"That all the people of the earth might know the hand of the LORD, that it is mighty: that ye might fear the LORD your God forever." Joshua 4:24

Lord, Your water cycle system for this world is incredible! Ocean to cloud to rain to rivers and back to ocean in never ending consistency$_5$. As if the molecular structure of water, H2O, isn't amazing enough. Water is the only liquid that expands when frozen and is lighter than its liquid state$_5$. This allows water resources to be preserved on land and the organisms within it to be safe underneath a protective layer of ice in the winter$_5$. How wonderful Lord that You created water as a substance that protects us and sustains us in every way. Water protects us from extreme heat like indulging in a refreshing lake dive or kids devouring popsicles. Water protects us from deep cold by insulating the land and our homes. Water nourishes and revives every square millimeter of our body and makes up roughly 60 % of our body$_5$. Your masterful molecular creation functions precisely as You ordered. "He hath made the earth by his power, and he hath established the world by his wisdom, and hath stretched out the heaven by his understanding. When he uttered his voice, there is a multitude of waters in the heavens; and he causeth the vapours to ascend from the ends of the earth: he maketh lightnings with rain, and bringeth forth the wind out of His treasures." Jeremiah 51:15-17

Lamb of God, our souls adore Thee,

While upon Thy Face we gaze,

There the Father's love and glory

Shine in all their brightest rays.

Thy Almighty power and wisdom

All creation's works proclaim,

Heaven and earth alike confess Thee,

As the ever great I Am.

(Hymn 27, A few Hymns and some Spiritual Songs selected 1856 for The Little Flock)[18]

Oh God, You are the Great I Am!

Terrible, wonderful, fire and water,

Creator, Sustainer, Lion and Lamb

Holy Light shrouded in darkness

Oh God, You are The Great I Am!

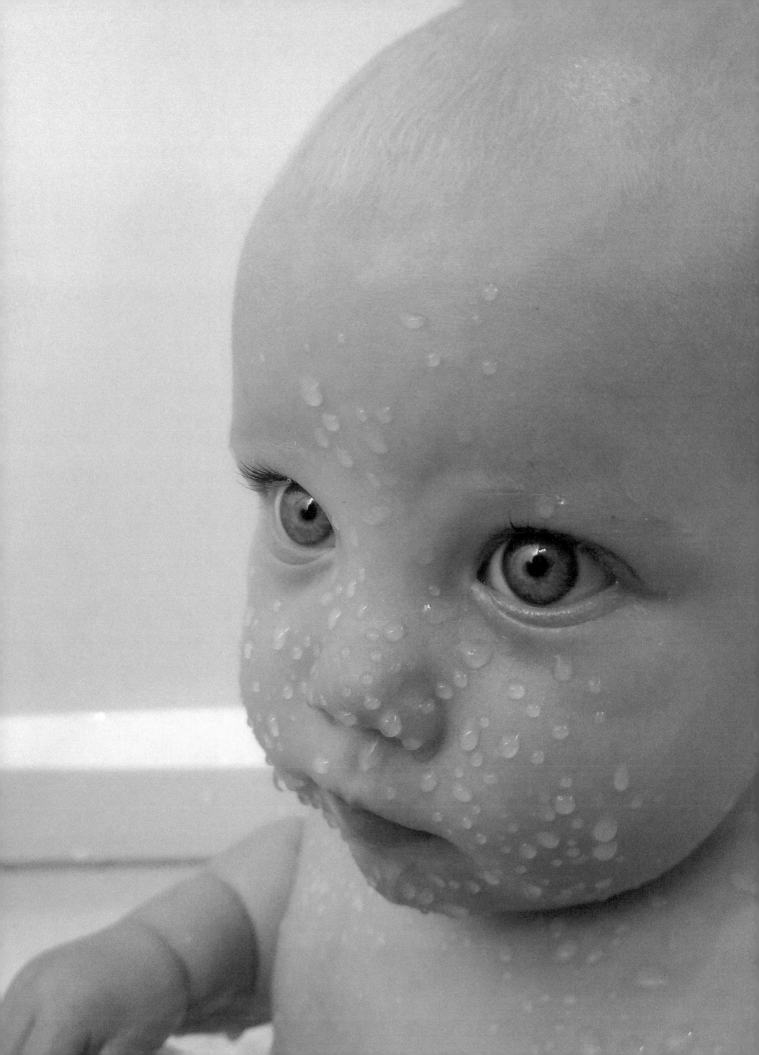

Thank You Lord

Thank you Lord for the rain
For the sky
For the pain
Who am I?
To receive blood's bought stain?
Sing Hallelujah, Hallelujah, Hallelujah
To the world so sweet
So they want to sit at His feet
And bask in His glory around
Sing Hallelujah, Hallelujah, Hallelujah
Thank you Lord for the sun
For the clouds
As they run
Little mounds
In Your heavenly blue.
Thank you Lord for a heart
For a mind
To impart
Blessed Truth
From Your heavenly Word
Sing Hallelujah, Hallelujah, Hallelujah
To the world so sweet
So they want to sit at His feet
And bask in His glory around
Sing Hallelujah, Hallelujah, Hallelujah

"And God said, Let the earth bring forth grass, the herb yielding seed, and the fruit tree yielding fruit after his kind, whose seed is in itself, upon the earth: and it was so."

Genesis 1:11

"Blessed is the man that walketh not in the counsel of the ungodly, nor standeth in the way of sinners, nor sitteth in the seat of the scornful. But His delight is in the law of the LORD; and in his law doth he meditate day and night. And he shall be like a tree planted by the rivers of water, that bringeth forth his fruit in his season; his leaf also shall not wither; and whatsoever he doeth shall prosper." Psalm 1:1-3

Lord, you are so concerned about life reproducing in every organism. May we feel the contagious wonder at seeing organisms grow physically and humans grow spiritually. Everything You have created Lord is an example of Your Word and Your Ways. May the new life You have given us in the death of Your Only Begotten Son be the fuel to produce more spiritual seeds of love towards others. The plants in this world give all of their energy and life to continue the DNA You have given them by producing seeds each year. You have not only given each human enough DNA to stretch to the sun and back 100 times[1], but sin free DNA with eternal life in heaven if we will only accept it. May our delight in Your Word fuel a roaring passion to share Your fruits of the Spirit with others. We have only one life to give and its shortness demands extreme sacrifice in putting all our energy into planting Your Words of Love into the fallow heart ground of ones who are around us. Lord, we don't deserve the life giving water of refreshing peace and love You have bestowed on us, but rather may our hearts only desire be to pass it on to the next generation.

He is the Alpha and Omega
The beginning and the end.
He knows our life and purpose
To this world us He sends.

Yes Lord! You are Mighty!
Yes Lord! You are True!
Yes Lord! I want to be devoted to You!

Teach me
To live as the lilies
Graced in Your beauty and love.
Shew me
How to love everyone
For we were all created from above.
Bring me
The secret of compassion
To bring lost souls in need.
Love me
For I am loveless
Full of sin and human greed.
Save me
A place under Your wing
Where amidst storm and gale I can sing.

"And the earth brought forth grass, and herb yielding seed after his kind, and the tree yielding fruit, whose seed was in itself, after his kind: and God saw that it was good."

Genesis 1:12

"That ye might walk worthy of the Lord unto all pleasing, being fruitful in every good work, and increasing in the knowledge of God; Strengthened with all might, according to his glorious power, unto all patience and longsuffering with joyfulness;" Colossians 1:10-11

Lord, thank you for the privilege of being made in Your Image. We are infinitesimally small and weak and yet You grant us the opportunity to display the fruits of Your Spirit. "But the fruit of the Spirit is love, joy, peace, longsuffering, gentleness, goodness, faith, meekness, temperance: against such there is no law." (Galatians 5:22) However tainted these fruits in our lives are with the funguses of our fleshly sin You grant us the remedies in Your Word. Oh how each of us desire the peaceable fruits of righteousness and yet it is impossible in our own strength. Save us Lord each day from our sinful selves and grant the new man You grafted in our hearts strength to grow and flourish. Water our hearts with Your Word and shine your Love upon us so we may grow to be more Christ-like. Lord, as we become more Christ-like and reach towards heaven, the world around us will be watching for flaws and inconsistencies. May we have a drop of Your Power to be patient and loving and joyful no matter the circumstances around us. Your longsuffering with us is an example of what we should be to our peers. May we be so caught up with looking heavenward that our fruits of the Spirit be only noticed by the ones who grab ahold of them to survive. This is our calling to grow in Christ-likeness and produce fruit (spiritual nourishment) for this generation and seeds (spiritual regeneration) for the future. Then God will be able to say, "Well done, thou good and faithful servant: thou hast been faithful over a few things, I will make thee ruler over many things: enter thou into the joy of thy lord." Matthew 25:21

Guard Your Own

O God, in whom we live and move,
Without whom life were death—
We bring Thee those in whom Thy love
Has breathed the living Breath.
O make them, keep them sensitive
In pure obedience;
In all they do, in all they give,
Be love and reverence.

(By Amy Carmichael) [17]

You open my heart
Carefully, lovingly, easily.
I trust
Your time.
You fill me with spirits
Love, joy, peace,
I sing of you.
Your love encompasses me
Strong, true, unchangeable
I cry
For joy.

"And the evening and the morning were the third day." Genesis 1:13

"And very early in the morning the first day of the week, they came unto the sepulcher at the rising of the sun." Mark 16:2

Lord, You are RISEN!!! No human action could delay You from rising the third day in triumph over the grave. Our hearts can't fathom the power that speaks things into existence submitting Itself to a perverse creation such as we are. You who set this whole universe in motion, creating time, chemical compounds, gravity, light, atoms and all the physical aspects of the matter around us; DIED. The number three in Your Word means divine fullness or completion, perfection in testimony. On the third day, after fully bowing Your Holiness into human shoes, the Trinity called ARISE! You, our LORD JESUS CHRIST have completed in perfection the testimony of God's unwavering love towards His ever wavering and sinful people. May we never hesitate to be as passionate as Mary Magdalene in her all-consuming love for the Master. May we rise early in the morning on the first day of the week and remember Your Divine and Perfect Love for us. May our hearts worship You in all the fullness of reverence and fear each day as we realize that someday the Trinity will call us home to heaven too. As the sun rises in glory and brightness each morning, may it warm our hearts to know without a shadow of a doubt that HE IS RISEN! HE is ALIVE FOREVER MORE!

Lord, I love to hear Your voice

As it floats on the wind

Though the trees and meadows

I wish I had never sinned.

You called to me, I answered

With tears and thoughts of myself

Why am I so selfish?

Christians give, not take for self.

I can't believe You love me

There is nothing here to love

All is rusted with sin and greed

I Praise You Lord! That I'll

be with You above!!!

"**And God said, Let there be lights in the firmament of the heaven to divide the day from the night; and let them be for signs, and for seasons, and for days, and years:**" Genesis 1:14

"**Let your light so shine before men, that they may see your good works, and glorify your Father which is in heaven.**" Matthew 5:16

Lord, thank you for the testimony of the night sky as we see the patterns of Your creativity played out in the detail before us each time we look up. Only You would have perfectly planned the chemistry of the moon to reflect our sun and thus become a perpetual night light. Only You could create the star of David to rest over Bethlehem the night Your Son, Our Lord Jesus Christ, was born into this world. Lord, You created and know the constellation patterns above each continent, every season of the year. You created the sun in its unimaginable intensity to produce enough energy to heat this world to a perfect and livable temperature range every day. You created this world to orbit not only the sun, but also on its own axis. This gives almost all areas of this world and opportunity to grow plants at different times. These plants rid our earth of toxic carbon dioxide by absorbing it and grant us life-sustaining oxygen in return. This orbit of the earth is the inspiration for our yearly calendar as the night sky magnifies different aspects of Your creation each month. May or hearts magnify Your Glory as well each day and night. No matter how small the task may seem, may You Father of Light be praised. No matter how insignificant we think we are, may You Father of Love be praised. No matter what opportunities we have, may You Father of Glory be praised in them.

This little light of mine,
I'm gonna let it shine!
This little light of mine,
I'm gonna let it shine!
Everyday, everyday,
Everyday and everyway.
I'm gonna let my little light shine!

(Lyric by Ernie and Debby Rettino) [22]

38

Each new moment is a gift from Your hand
To praise You at the top of lungs while we can
No shyness or selfish are allowed on this trip
To holiness we go and in fiery baptism dip.

"And let them be for lights in the firmament of the heaven to give light upon the earth: and it was so." Genesis 1:15

"What I tell you in darkness, that speak ye in light: and what ye hear in the ear, that preach ye upon the housetops." Matthew 10:27

Lord, what a fearful thing to be reminded that You breathed out the fireball of nuclear energy called the sun and the acid fireball we call Saturn. These planets give off light as a by-product of the chemical reactions encompassing their surface. Without the sun's obedience to Your command no living thing would survive on our planet. May we consider our faithful walk in this world in light of the planets. Our obedience to walk by faith and proclaim God's light is critical to souls surviving on this planet and into an eternal heaven. Just as we experience a typical and physical sixteen-hour day and an eight hour night, on average; we will also experience times in our life where darkness overcomes our joy. Remember, darkness is a time of refreshment for the body as it absorbs the energy and nutrients needed to fully function. Even in the darkest of nights there are still stars uncalculated light years away shining light into our atmosphere for God's Glory. May we take the quiet and dark hours of disappointment, grief, betrayal, physical ailment etc. and gather gems from Christ to give away in the light. White light is a combination of all colors combined in purity. May our light be pure and well balanced in the colors of Your Glory Jesus as we proclaim Your Love. As beacons of light from a lighthouse over the rough shoreline, may we faithfully light the pathway to salvation for anyone who comes near.

"Go tell it on the mountain,
over the hills and everywhere.
Go, tell it on the mountain,
that Jesus Christ is born!"
(lyric refrain by John Wesley Work 1865) [23]

I love You Lord
And I lift my voice
To worship You
Oh, my soul, rejoice!
Take joy my King
In what You hear
Let it be a sweet, sweet sound
In Your Ear.
(Lyric by Petra) [20]

"And God made two great lights; the greater light to rule the day, the lesser light to rule the night: he made the stars also." Genesis 1:16

"In him was life; and the life was the light of men. And the light shineth in darkness; and the darkness comprehended it not. There was a man sent from God, whose name was John. The same came for a witness, to bear witness of the Light, that all men though him might believe. " John 1:4-7

Lord, thank you for the sacrifice of Your only begotten Son. The cherished One of the Father given in love to rescue a filthy and hopelessly corrupt race. Without You Lord, there is only darkness within our hearts and an unquenchable void. Thank you for piercing the darkness as those soldier's pierced Your side Jesus. As we as humans gave up entirely on ever having a Saviour, You smiled and in three days we finally saw Your greatest miracle. Jesus became the divine fullness and completion of Your Salvation plan and thus became the Light of the world. May our eyes be ever watching each day to follow in Jesus' footsteps and walk faithfully. Lord, we know that You created

Satan too and he prefers to rule in darkness. May we not be deceived as he often reflects a little of the light and power of God but pointed in the opposite direction. The moon has a few similar attributes that it rules the night, and reflects the suns powerful light. It also has no water which reminds us of the deadness of our lives without You Lord the Water of Life. May we never forget that the closer we get to You the Son of God and the physical sun, the more overwhelming are the light and all-consuming power. The closer we get to Satan and the moon, the deeper the darkness and coldness of lack of life. May our lives be like the stars in the many unfathomable miles their lights shine for Your Glory. We have no idea Lord in what direction You may choose to shine Your love within us. May we be obedient to Your calling. May the world see a glimmer of Jesus when they see us from afar. Satan's darkness could not and will not overcome Jesus, the Light of the World! Neither will Satan have any power to quench our vibrant testimony. The Holy Spirit You gave us is alive and powerful in our hearts and like the sun will dispel the forces of darkness around us. Even in the event of a star dying, the light it emits continues on through space for eternity. God's personal witness of Jesus Christ was John the Baptist. His bold testimony was "...Behold, the Lamb of God, which taketh away the sin of the world." John 1:29 His words in the Spirit live on for eternity as a record of his faithfulness amidst adversity, obedience, and extreme temptation. John promised the coming Saviour who would dispel the darkness of sin. God, you created the stars as a promise of the soon coming daybreak. May we live as a promise of the soon coming return of Jesus and our feeble light pierce the darkness of the sinful world we live in.

Shine, Jesus, shine;

fill this land with the Father's Glory.

Blaze, Spirit, blaze;

Set our hearts on fire.

Flow, river, flow;

Flood the nations with grace and mercy.

Send forth Your Word,

Lord, and let there be light."

(lyric by Graham Kendrick 1987) [20]

Freedom's Path

Whoever thought that life would be this way

The constant push of truth and the pull of evil sway

The breath of God created the Garden of Eden pure

The breath of Satan began sin's deadly, constant lure

The love of Adam and Eve created Able out of grace

The wrath of Satan through Cain slew him in God's face

Noah obeyed God's voice and made an ark of wood

Then in his tent exposed, his son looked and stood

Moses served the Lord and rescued God's inheritance

The devil wanting Moses' body defied the Lord's stance

Solomon talked with God and He granted his request

But foolish women and riches stole all his wisdom's best

David reigned in passion and all was victory

Until he let lust begin the end of his story.

But...BUT...BUT!!!!

The story of God's power and love doesn't end up there

He sent a Redeemer to corrupt the devil's dark lair.

No more does Satan have the last word!

No more does he have power

No more do we have to succumb

Or to his temptations cower

For we have a Redeemer

A lover and friend

Who laid down His life

For all without end.

His blood has the antibodies
to kill sin and greed,
And anything else
The devil may feed.
Hurray!!!!! We have victory
Hurray!!!!! We don't have to give up
Hurray!!!!! We can finish our story
In drinking Jesus' cup
Freedom from fear, doubt and dismal decay
We have a way out! No matter what may
We command the evil one to leave us alone
In Jesus Name and the Power
of His Precious Blood!
He has to obey the Greatest Power known.
For the evil one is DEFEATED!
He has lost his game
Now we can be seated
By Jesus the same.
Glory Hallelujah!!!!! Jesus is our King
Glory Hallelujah!!!!! Jesus lives again
Glory Hallelujah!!!!! Angels do sing
Freedom had finally come to men again.

"And God set them in the firmament of the heaven to give light upon the earth." Genesis 1:17

"By the Word of the Lord were the heavens made, and all the host of them by the breath of his mouth." Psalm 33:6

Lord, You have set us here on earth to give light to the hurting and lost treasured souls around us. Unlike the stars and sun our obedience is a choice daily and hourly. Please grant our feeble hearts and minds the strength to persevere in absolute obedience to Your commands for each day of our lives. Like the moon, may our faces shine brightly of Your attributes as we look always to Your radiant Love and Light. With Your breath You created this universe of universes, plankton, planets, platypuses, elephants, salmon, worms, and redwood forests. If we reflect You, what do we create with our breath? Jealousy? Pornography? Hatred? Nothing? Can we support abortion which is the killing of souls and still reflect? OH LORD, help us! Help us! Help us to be a light, an all-consuming powerful light of Your righteousness, love, humbleness, forgiveness, truth and joy. We are and were created by the breath of Your lips to sing your praises NO matter the circumstances. Scientifically our brains are smarter and free of mental illness if we just obey and ""In everything give thanks: for this is the will of God in Christ Jesus concerning you." I Thessalonians 5:18 May we endure to the end of our lives with truth and righteousness. Then we will hear those blessed words, "Well done thou good and faithful servant!"

Lord of Glory
You are so real to me.
I reach with my heart
And absorb Your love.
You are endless...
I only a speck
Time...what is it?
Nothing compared to eternity with You.

May this passion be to You
For who loves us with such grace?
Lord in everything we do
May we shine your blessed face!

"And to rule over the day and over the night, and to divide the light from the darkness: and God saw that it was good." Genesis 1:18

"Therefore my people shall know my name: therefore they shall know in that day that I am he that doth speak: behold, it is I." Isaiah 52:6

God of all creation, You are the sustainer of all life day and night. May we consider Your greatness and power that You rule with in such peace. Rule over our wayward and selfish hearts Lord! Remove the darkness of sin from our inner being and cast it where we can't retrieve it. For darkness is our nature to prowl and hunt all Your creation under Your wing. May we be freed from its grips and FINALLY trust You Father to give us our meat in due season while we walk in the light. Please speak to us Lord as we try to find our way. May our lives be a blessing to You as we patiently wait the perfection of Christ-likeness. Please faithfully remove darkness from our souls. In that glorious day when we will glide upward towards Your perfect and all-satisfying light and love; we will declare for eternity Your every perfection. For God, who commanded the light to shine out of darkness, hath shined in our hearts, to give the light of the knowledge of the glory of God in the face of Jesus Christ." II Corinthians 4:6

"And God saw that it was good..."

The Light of the world was a part of the Godhead creating light.

Light was spoken into being by a triune God to illuminate the darkness.

Darkness fled from the mouth of God to reveal the canvas of Creation.

Creation blossomed and grew with plants and trees exalting God's creative genius.

Genius of God spilled into the insects, mammals and all creatures.

Creatures exemplified the attributes of God and honored God in obedience.

Obedience was key to the success of the created Eden Paradise.

Paradise was shattered by the sin of man forever tainting his genetic line with sin.

Sin's consequence was death and separation from God forever.

Forever was Christ's agape love for humanity

Humanity rejected the love of Christ and crucified Jesus, "The Lamb of God."

"The Lamb of God" in laying down his life dissolved the darkness of our souls.

Souls wanting to be freed accepted into their hearts "The Light of the World."

"The Light of the World" is a part of the Godhead creating light.

"And the evening and the morning were the fourth day." Genesis 1:19

"Now among these were of the children of Judah, Daniel, Hananiah, Mishael, and Azariah." Daniel 1:6

Lord, we know that the number four means completeness in creation and the ordination of God. Creation was complete without us humans, but You chose us Lord. You chose us to be vessels of praise and adoration for eternity. You were not satisfied with the physical elements of the earth glorifying Your Name day in and day out as they obediently followed Your laws of gravity and thermodynamics while applying Your manuscript of DNA. Your plans are infinitely grander than we can comprehend and widened by the command of God to include creatures such as us filled with hate, lust, and greed. God, why would You choose creatures whose fleshly nature despises the grandeur of I AM to be a bride for Your Son? May our hearts be transformed to proclaim faithfully Your love to the world. As the four children of Israel, may we not be ashamed to stand firm in declaring that You are the ONE and ONLY True God of all creation. "If it be so, our God whom we serve is able to deliver us from the burning fiery furnace, and he will deliver us out of thine hand, O king. But if not, be it known unto thee, O king, that we will not serve thy gods, nor worship the golden image which thou hast set up." Daniel 3:17-18 The maker of all atoms. May we choose You and choose life.

Choose Life! I cry
As the babies die
More millions than I can comprehend
Choose Life! He sighed
On the cross He died
His blood, sins curse of death He did mend.

Oh baby dear!
Please don't shed another tear
For heaven
Is your home now
Killed by mother
Doctor, and father
With a sword.
We cry, O Lord!

"And they cried with a loud voice, saying, How long, O Lord, holy and true, dost thou not judge and avenge our blood…?" Revelation 6:10

"And God said, Let the waters bring forth abundantly the moving creature that hath life, and the fowl that may fly above the earth in the open firmament of heaven." Genesis 1:20

"Then the Levites, Jeshua, and Kadmiel, Bani, Hashabniah, Sherebiah, Hodijah, and Shebaniah, and Pethahiah, said, Stand up and bless the LORD your God for ever and ever: and blessed be thy glorious name, which is exalted above all blessing and praise. Thou, even thou, art LORD alone; thou hast made heaven, the heaven of heavens, with all their host, the earth, and all things that are therein, the seas, and all that is therein, and thou preservest them all; and the host of heaven worshippeth thee." Nehemiah 9:5-6

"And God said…" 2546 times in Your Word. What a blessing to be the benefactor of Your words Lord! We can enjoy the oceans and streams full of plankton, salmon, and even platypus to show Your sense of humor and design. Your creatures are so varied and complicated that after thousands of years of human thought we still cannot match the movements of a simple dragonfly or hummingbird with a machine. Nor can we fully explain why the largest fish, a whale shark, survives one hundred percent on the smallest prey in the ocean, plankton. We think of Your fine balance as birds like gannets are programmed by Your words to hurl themselves from as high as 130 feet in the air into the depths of the ocean to correctly catch their food$_6$. How could they ever catch a frantically moving fish in a school with the factor of light refraction? Only You Lord could create and teach that delicate balance. May we be bold as these men of old to stand up in front of our peers of today and proclaim with confidence and assurance Your Power and Truth. May we have such confidence in Your plan that we can hurl ourselves into whatever calling You've given. Should we ever be afraid of another human who will die like us? NO! Praise Him all ye people! Tell others of the miracles you have seen and heard. Worship the God that will make you soar up to the heavens more elegantly than a butterfly and faster than a hummingbird.

Naught separates us
'cept sin for a awhile.
Still You love me
No matter the mile.

Your Love is
Deeper than the oceans
Wider than the biggest sea
Vaster than our universe
What is my love to Thee?

"And God created great whales, and every living creature that moveth, which the waters brought forth abundantly, after their kind, and every winged fowl after his kind: and God saw that it was good."
Genesis 1:21

"But take diligent heed to do the commandment and the law, which Moses the servant of the LORD charged you, to love the LORD your God, and to walk in all his ways, and to keep his commandments, and to cleave unto him, and to serve him with all your heart and with all your soul." Joshua 22:5

What a pleasure to serve You the One and Only True God who could create the delicate balance of creation! We know how much work it is to keep a little aquarium going with pH, microorganisms, predator vs. prey, plants etc. How incredible You are to keep this world going and the creativity involved is beyond our comprehension. You created the creatures of the sea as an integral part of the circle of life all over this planet. How can a loggerhead turtle build her first nest in the very same beach she was born in twenty years ago[8]? How amazing to see a peacock flounder or a cuttlefish instantly change different colors and their body transforms to odd shapes to avoid predator detection. Even the minute blind shrimp and the goby fish follow Your plan to build and protect a burrow together. Why aren't they predator and prey? Only You know Lord. Your ways are infinitely complex and perfectly balanced as we see the relationships between Your creatures that You have ordained. Do the angels look on in awe of the way we are made and how we interact with each other and our world? We are the only creatures with a soul and are given the choice to serve and exalt Him. Will you dedicate your life to His plan? It may be hard. A parent Emperor penguin walks two 50 mile excursions each year without a meal to feed its one baby chick[7]. An artic tern travels 25,000 miles from Greenland to Antarctica every year being an average of .25lb in weight[6]. Lord You made each creature for its direct purpose and with special talents to magnify Your creative glory and power. What is our personal purpose? What are our personal gifts? Are we obeying the words of Moses and no matter what storms assail us in our journey are we being victorious in coming through? Sea creatures have an advantage in huge storms to just sink deeper into the water and the storm rages on over them and they are safe and secure. In the storms of our lives we too can just sink deeper into the living water Your Word and be safe and secure no matter the drama in life. The fowl are given a way to overcome storms too by flying above them or out of them. What a comfort that anytime life gets too rough for us all we need to do is look heavenward and spread our wings in faith. God, You will grant us the wings of faith to overcome the perils of life whenever we seek to love and serve Your Holiness.

> *Do you have faith? Do you have love?*
> *Do you have faith wings, and soaring above?*
> *Oh God You are gracious. Oh God You are true*
> *Help us Your children, in everything we do*

"And God blessed them, saying be fruitful, and multiply, and fill the waters in the seas, and let fowl multiply in the earth." Genesis 1:22

"It is of the LORD's mercies that we are not consumed, because his compassions fail not. They are new every morning: great is they faithfulness." Lamentations 3:22-23

With the breath of Your holy mouth and the Love of Your holy heart You created creatures to live in that salty brine we call ocean. The water filled ocean is a symbolic picture of You, Jesus. "… they have forsaken me the fountain of living waters…" Jeremiah 2:13 We are symbolized by the "salt of the earth" Matthew 5:13. When we humans dissolve our lives into You the Living Water; then the possibilities for abundant life are endless. Practically speaking, You have modeled that for us in placing the effortless gliding stingray, giant 6 foot clam$_9$, phytoplankton that make 50 percent of our oxygen$_{10,}$ and seahorses in our teaming oceans. A dizzying array of Your handiwork multiplying and following the food chain in harmony and consistency. What came first? Was it the largest animal on the planet the 40 foot whale shark or the tiny plankton they feed on$_7$? Once again what came first? Was it the salmon eggs in the freshwater rivers or the salmon adults in the salty Pacific Ocean$_{11}$? God said… and it was so and is so as the incredible codependent balance of our world was created and continues today. Only of You Lord, can life exist and may we be diligent to fulfill our purpose while we are still alive on the earth. We may live only a month in the womb or for one hundred twenty years. You have dictated each life on this earth and spoken to them of their purpose. You are compassionate Lord in giving us one more day. "Are not five sparrows sold for two farthings, and not one of them is forgotten before God? But even the hairs of your head are all numbered. Fear not therefore: ye are of more value than many sparrows." (Luke 12:6&7) Please speak to us Lord and have compassion on us as we learn Your calling on our life. May our life suspended in Yours not prevent the fish and fowl to obey God's command to them to be fruitful and multiply. May our life dissolved into You be one of supporting abundant life in this world and in the world to come. It is never too late to obey because Your compassions fail not.

> Great is Thy faithfulness, O God my Father,
> There is no shadow of turning with Thee;
> Thou changest not, Thy compassions, they fail not;
> As Thou hast been, Thou forever will be.
> Great is Thy faithfulness!
> Great is Thy faithfulness!
> Morning by morning new mercies I see.
> All I have needed Thy hand hath provided;
> Great is Thy faithfulness, Lord, unto me!
> (lyric by Thomas Chisholm 1923) $_{12}$

As a sparrow on the wind,
High, confident free
With the earth beneath my wings
The Son before me.
I trust You Lord for everything
Food, raiment and friends.
Sufficient for me is You,
Whatever God sends.
Lord, Almighty friend of mine
I cleave to You alone.
Your image may I reflect
Watering seeds sown.
I soar as high as mountains
Visit valleys of woe.
But Lord You are beside me
Wherever I go
You are a blessing in my life
Dear and closest Friend.
Forever I will cherish You, Lord
Even till the end.

El Shaddai, El Shaddai
All-Sufficient One
Who am I? Who am I?
My beloved one
El Shaddai, El Shaddai
Nourisher and Guide
Where am I? Where am I?
Right by My side

"And the evening and the morning were the fifth day." Genesis 1:23

"But take diligent heed to do the commandment and the law, which Moses the servant of the LORD charged you, to love the LORD your God, and to walk in all his ways, and to keep his commandments, and to cleave unto him, and to serve him with all your heart and with all your soul. So Joshua blessed them, and sent them away: and they went unto their tents." Joshua 22: 5&6

Lord, why is it that after You speak here on this world then darkness sets in for a time? Is it that You are just holding Your breath in anticipation of Your instructions to be carried out before declaring the next step? Joshua in the Spirit of God declared our next step after Your establishment of the Isrealite nation. "But take diligent heed to do the commandment and the law, which Moses the servant of the LORD charged you, to love the LORD your God, and to walk in all his ways, and to keep his commandments, and to cleave unto him, and to serve him with all your heart and with all your soul." Is that so little to ask when the Creator of the Universe is speaking? Joshua commanded and blessed the people. Oh Lord, may the blessings and commandments of God flow out of our mouths as we diligently speak Your Word to the next generation. Please help us to adequately teach our children and equip them to be able to rule their own homes someday in Your Spirit. Are we being fruitful and multiplying physically and spiritually like God has commanded? Lord, you are holding our every breath. You speak light and then love like a parent. As the Creator You will speak the fire of consequence to those who don't heed Your Words and quit destroying Your creation. Will we be found obedient no matter the time of day or night?

I am just a young child what can I do?
Others are bigger and eloquent too.
Please fill my mouth with words of You
Spirit led and holy true.

At the ending of my day
May there be fruit not just play
For in heaven I want to stay
My body is Yours no matter what may.

"And God said, Let the earth bring forth the living creature after his kind, cattle, and creeping thing, and beast of the earth after his kind: and it was so." Genesis 1:24

"It is a fearful thing to fall into the hands of the living God." Hebrews 10:31

Dear Lord Jesus Christ! We have sinned! We have disrespected Your loving and creative hand that blesses and provides for all Your creatures. Woe to us as we have killed your creatures for sport and plundered their habitats in our selfishness. We have demolished the majority of habitats for our green lawns and parking lots. We have traded the pictures and movies of a place for the real thing. Even the worms and insects are important to You and You have given them the greatest jobs here in this world. Turning dead and decaying plant material back into nutrient rich compost for the next generation to thrive in$_{13}$. If Your mouth is that powerful how unimaginable is the Power of Your hands that act out the power of Your words. Woe to us who abuse the creation of God. There will be consequences for upsetting the insect food sources of songbirds and inoculating the herbs of the earth that were given to us for food$_{14}$. "How long shall the land mourn, and the herbs of every field wither, for the wickedness of them that dwell therein? the beasts are consumed, and the birds; because they said, He shall not see our last end." (Jeremiah 12:4) There will be repercussions for driving species to extinction or limiting their range to zoo walls. May we as stewards of the earth, Lord, learn to care for Your Creation and not carelessly consume it upon our lust. "It is a fearful thing to fall into the hands of the living God," (Hebrews 10:31) UNLESS we obey.

We are caretakers for our Master
While He is away
There are many details
But He is our stay
We are to bear abundant fruit
In this life and the life to come
With love and Respect for all creatures
Not pretending we are dumb.
Ignorance is not bliss
As everyone knows
We are still responsible
For what each of us sows

"And God made the beast of the earth after his kind, and cattle after their kind, and everything that creepeth upon the earth after his kind: and God saw that it was good." Genesis 1:25

"And the Spirit of the LORD will come upon thee, and thou shalt prophesy with them, and shalt be turned into another man." I Samuel 10:6

Oh Thou Creator and Sustainer of Life and Love and Light. Even after seeing all the good things You created on that day like the dog, mouse, kangaroo, cow, moose, panda bear and centipede; it is unbelievable You could still think of more to create. Your creativity is boundless and invigorating as we learn more and more each year about the details in each organism. Somehow we think You were done creating after that intense week of creation, but You were just beginning. Life unfolded in the weeks and months ahead. Caterpillars turned into butterflies and lambs turned into sheep. Thus You began the arduous journey of shepherding and creating Christians within a sinful world. We begin much like monarch caterpillars as they devour toxic milkweed all day long$_{15}$. We are greedy for food and stuff to consume and with little to no regard of You Lord or Your Ways. Our only thoughts are for ourselves and our toxic food we relish called sin. Then You give us a God moment where we like the caterpillar humble ourselves to Your will and rest from our strivings to submit. The Holy Spirit indwells us to create a new man in us. A new focus. Sometimes that moment feels like our world is turned upside down as we hang onto the new thread of hope that You Jesus are our Savior and Lord. May we even assume the upside down position of the caterpillar in the shape of a "J" as we wait for Your calling$_{15}$. You will completely dissolve the old man and create a new man in us. Like metamorphosis, this rebirth will develop in us the wings of faith to go heavenward. Soon we be free from this life on earth and will fly away to the heavens to be with You. No more will we taste of toxic sin. No more will we be cumbered with excess weight nor have to worry about falling. No more will we be alone, but God will provide a safe haven for his children to rest together in Glory. May You, God the Father, God the Son, and the Holy Spirit finally be able to rest from all your labors in the years to come; and see that the metamorphosis of sinful humans to sanctified humans was good.

God we seek Your transformation

Our souls are empty

without You

Nothing fills, not

even occupation

A black hole, it is true

Turn us upside down

Do whatever it will take

For in our sins we'll drown

In the burning lake

"And God said, Let us make man in our image, after our likeness: and let them have dominion over the fish of the sea, and over the fowl of the air, and over the cattle, and over all the earth, and over every creeping thing that creepeth upon the earth." Genesis 1:26

"And the God of peace shall bruise Satan under your feet shortly. The grace of our Lord Jesus Christ be with you. Amen." Romans 16:20

Lord God Almighty, Your creation of man is astounding. A living, breathing, independent thinking, mass of 37.2 trillion cells working together in unison for a lifetime₁. To think that all the brains and all the computer systems of the world could never create even one of those cells from nothing. We are a walking and talking miracle every moment. What an honor to represent the Great I Am! We were put here on this earth to tend it and keep it in grace-filled dominion. In our dominance are we representing God or Satan? Do we seek and win trash for the landfills or do we seek and win souls? God gives us power over every creature of the earth, angels and even Satan. What are we doing with Your power Lord? How are we using our hands, feet, mind and mouth? "So then every one of us shall give account of himself to God." Romans 14:12 May we be filled with Your Spirit Lord Jesus and represent You in grace and bear Your image. Thank you for Your Spirit that allows us a relationship with You even with our imperfect flesh here on earth. Thank You for the hope of a soon coming marriage with You. Thank you for creating men to think like You in desiring honor, respect, appreciation for their labors, hierarchy and strength. It helps us to see Your likeness. Thank you also for creating women to be like You in desiring love, relationship, companionship, nurture and beauty. Together in marriage we personify You as our opposite personalities fit and work together to create a balance and a picture of all that You God are. A marriage of one man and one woman is powerful when they function together in the Spirit of God because it encapsulates God's total character. Woe to the demons around when a marriage is strong. Lord, You are our King! You are our Lord and we stand with You in the fight to bring souls to the safety of heaven before it is too late. We look to the day when Your Spirit will so fill us that we will have the strength and power to bruise Satan under our feet. In Jesus Name and in the Power of Jesus' Blood, Amen Amen

Heaven bound are we!!

Our Lord we shall see!

No more competition

For our changing affection.

No more consequences

Only fulfilled senses

No more illnesses

Only God kisses

Heaven bound are we!

Our Lord we shall see!

You are my all!
I will not forget Your loving call
That opens up my heart.
Without Your strength and love I do fall
But never to depart.
Unimaginable love, how vast
And how free to my heart.
At Your feet my vile self I cast
A new beginning I start.

Thank you seems inadequate to say
For all You've done for me.
But thank you for every breath and day
I lay them at Your feet.
Jesus, my Savior, my dear close friend
Thank you for walking with me.
With You I can enjoy every road bend
For demons from me flee.

"So God created man in his own image, in the image of God created he him; male and female created he them." Genesis 1:27

"And Adam lived a hundred and thirty years, and begat a son in his own likeness, after his image; and called his name Seth:" Genesis 5:3

(Jesus) "Who is the image of the invisible God, the firstborn of every creature:" Colossians 1:15

LORD God the Almighty, the firstborn of every creature. . . pause … You created us. Male and female as a relationship and partnership in visiting with their Creator. Two children of perfection living with their beloved Creator in a perfect world. Every animal was given a "teammate" in the circle of life. Each one necessary and gifted to help the other accomplish the task given to them by You. What gifts do we have as male and female that can strengthen each other in spirit, soul and body? Not just sex, but balances of fight and flight, aggressive and passive, leader and follower, adventuresome and routine, practical and visionary, people oriented and task oriented etc. etc. How can we build up the other to reach their potential and calling on their life by our Lord? The name Seth means "appointed" in Webster's Dictionary. Are our children appointed to carry on in the image of God? How can they if we don't take the appointment of God seriously and reflect God's new man in us? Oh God, please don't let us live a hundred and twenty years before there is any fruit born in our lives that resembles You. Now is the time and the time waits for no one. God, You became so frustrated with our human inability and disinterest in following Your commands of righteousness that You sent another man made in the image of the invisible God. Like any good farmer would do, You introduced a new pure strain of DNA to the original variety You decided to grow. Our human seed is hopelessly corrupt and cannot produce the fruit of righteousness anymore no matter the human effort. Jesus, You, remedied the overwhelming loss to sin. "Believe on the Lord Jesus Christ and thou shalt be saved." Acts 16:31 Now, like any good farmer, You keep only the seeds that are viable and true to the parentage of Christ. Human seeds cross-pollinated by a sin nature are like hybrid plant seeds. Only viable for one generation and then fit to be burned. This world is choking in the weeds of sin and soon You will burn it and start over like any practical farmer would do that doesn't want to destroy the soil composition and fertility. Oh Lord, we look forward to the day we can be planted in a new field called heaven and glorify You in perfection. "But now being made free from sin, and become servants to God, ye have your fruit unto holiness, and the end everlasting life." Romans 6:22

I raise my head
To view Your
radiant grace!
I open my mouth
To sing forever praise!
I move my hands
In service to my King!
I open my heart
For my Lord is amazing!

"And God blessed them, and God said unto them, Be fruitful, and multiply, and replenish the earth, and subdue it: and have dominion over the fish of the sea, and over the fowl of the air, and over every living thing that moveth upon the earth." Genesis 1:28

"And he answering said, Thou shalt love the Lord thy God with all thy heart, and with all thy soul, and with all thy strength, and with all thy mind; and thy neighbour as thyself." Luke 10:27

LORD, thank you for giving us this world to take care of. No matter if we are an ecologist, computer programmer, botanist, restaurant owner, biologist, mother, archeologist, shepherd or child: we are all called to replenish the earth. Replenish means in the Webster's Dictionary to fill with persons or animals: nourish: to fill or build up again. We are to have authority over this world with Your hand of love and respect. Who are we to abuse, and defame and deface the creative world that You made for us? Who are we to support the annihilation of millions of human babies[15.]? Who are we to engage in the annihilation of the bug, bee and weed population[14]? Who are we to allow a single company to control the food and seed population by creating hybrids and genetically altering the DNA of our food[14]? Genetically altered food isn't food. Even the bugs and animals know that and don't eat it. All the plants and animals are gifts, from You our Creator and given to build our health and strength. We are systematically killing ourselves and our future generations if we don't respect Your design. May our love and devotion and respect of You Lord spill over into the way we nourish our neighbors, the fish, the fowl, the soil and every living thing. It is our highest calling, our job, our love gift to our Creator and Friend. And in doing so we become a little bit more like You the Master Gardener every day. As we obey You, may we leave a legacy of Your image here in this world. What a calling to be a mirror of God to all the physical world. Oh Lord, help us!

Oh God, isn't that what Satan wanted all along?

To kill and maim creation and its song?

Our choice to serve the evil one

Look! LOOK! What it's done.

Our babies are killed, along with the bees

No children, no food, what's next? No seas?

No animal's, no insects, no plant's

No creation! I won! The evil one chants

But we will not give in or give up

For with Jesus we share His cup

His Grace and Healing will through us pour

We obey and proclaim, "I AM is the door"

"And God said, Behold, I have given you every herb bearing seed, which is upon the face of all the earth, and every tree, in the which is the fruit of a tree yielding seed; to you it shall be for meat." Genesis 1:29

"And the eyes of them both were opened, and they knew that they were naked; and they sewed fig leaves together, and made themselves aprons." Genesis 3:7

Lord, we are humbled by Your provision for Your first two children. Every tree and herb with its seed was given for meat in their yard. Our culture sets the standard for our yards to be lifeless of animals and bugs, fruitless and an almost empty land for our living space. We are despising Your provision of an oasis and trading it for chips and soda, roundup and crabgrass. Are we reaping the gifts You have so bountifully bestowed on the human race? It goes beyond apples and peaches to a complex interconnected ecosystem fully planned to be the beginning of replenishing the earth. Help us Lord to think of those weeds that crop up in the bare spots of the lawn as gifts from You our Creator. Dandelions are purifiers of the blood and kidneys when their leaves are eaten as salad greens, or their roots boiled for tea$_{19}$. They bring in pollinators consistently with their abundant flowers throughout the season$_{16}$. Their taproot breaks up packed soil so air, water, worms and healthy bacteria can inhabit infertile soil and replenish it$_{16}$. We are naked before You and humbled by our ignorance of Your plan and desire for abundant life in all areas we touch. That red clover we try so hard to eradicate is also a gift from You. Instead of taking nutrients out of the soil it puts nitrogen back in with the help of bacteria called mycorrhizae that live happily on its roots$_{16}$. If the blossoms are boiled for tea and consumed daily it has been known to put cancer in remission. It is also a good fodder for cattle and a strong producer of pollen packed blossoms. MMmmmm clover honey. If these are the lowly plants You have given us Lord and their benefits; there would not be enough gigabits available to handle the depths of Your blessings You created for us. May our eyes be opened to our failings and be passionate about changing our ways before it is too late. God, please give us wisdom and strength to do what is right the first time before the consequences are irreversible. "O

COME, let us sing unto the LORD; let us make a joyful noise to the rock of our salvation. Let us come before his presence with thanksgiving, and make a joyful noise unto him with psalms. For the LORD is a great God, and a great King above all gods. In his hand are the deep places of the earth: the strength of the hills is his also. The sea is his, and he made it: and his hands formed the dry land. O come, let us worship and bow down: let us kneel before the LORD our maker. For he is our God; and we are the people of his pasture, and the sheep of his hand. To day if you will hear his voice, Harden not your heart, as in the provocation, and as in the day of temptation in the wilderness:" Psalm 95: 1-8

Who is like unto the Lord of Hosts?

Who can make the rain fall down and the heat rise?

Who is like unto Jehovah-Jireh?

Who can make all knees bow and all souls arise?

Who is like unto the Great I AM?

Who can make all mountains fall and a new earth arise?

Take my eyes and let them be only looking Lord to Thee
Beholding glorious grace and love the center of my focus
Take my ears and let them be only hearing Lord of Thee.
Sweetest words I will ever hear "Father, It is finished."
Take my lips and let them be only voicing Lord of Thee
Singing praises continually, overflowing joy.
Take my feet and let them be firmly set to follow Thee
Over mountains and valleys, deep in the shadow of Your Love
Take my heart and let it be totally focused Lord on Thee
May the love that Jesus gave permeate my heart.
Take my hands and let them be only working Lord for thee
Created Lord to serve thee, they are for You alone.
Take my life and may it be fully devoted Lord to Thee.
For what is my life, Lord, without You right by my side?

Oh, bring forth thy bud, fair garden;
Sing, ye birds, jubilantly.
Lord of gardens-it is He
Walketh these green leafy ways-
Lord of buds and singing birds,
Even He, Rabboni.

(by Amy Carmichael)17

Who is like unto Thee?
The object of my affection.
The One who created all.
Divine love and correction.

"O God, thou art my God; early will I seek thee: my soul thirsteth for thee, my flesh longeth for thee in a dry and thirsty land, where no water is: To see thy power and glory, so as I have seen thee in the sanctuary. Because thy lovingkindness is better than life, my lips shall praise thee. Thus will I bless thee while I live: I will lift up my hands in thy name." Psalm 63:1-4

"And to every beast of the earth, and to every fowl of the air, and to everything that creepeth upon the earth, wherein there is life, I have given every green herb for meat: and it was so." Genesis 1:30

"Every moving thing that liveth shall be meat for you; even as the green herb have I given you all things." Genesis 9:3

Lord, there must have been incredible leisure and lack of fear in the garden of Eden. We have no idea what it is to walk in total confidence of our safety amongst Komodo dragons, snakes, tigers, mosquitos, wolves, hornets, lions, and even dinosaurs back then before sin. Many books are written on the amazing and unusual interspecies relationships found all over the world. It is funny that we still desire what would have been commonplace in the Garden of Eden. To have no predators or prey and no violence, but only perfect peace and tranquility. There is a part in all of us that wants to go back to that perfect Paradise and experience it for ourselves. And yet there are so many things Lord in your world now that we can implement and experience the blessings you intended in the Garden of Eden. We can eat the green herbs and plants of the field that you made and let them heal our bodies like they were created for. Lovage and all its parts fresh or dried is excellent for preventing winter illnesses. Peppermint grows wild in many ecosystems because it is helpful for all parts of the body. What rest and peace You bring Lord when I can just go shopping in the yard for the food I need. A handful of ripe raspberries off the vine and a sweet honeysuckle for the flitting child. A sweet potato out of the flowerpot and sprinkled chives from the front flower bed. The sun soaking rich vitamin D into my skin to fight viruses as I collect the treasures you have created. Sunflowers are not just pretty but keep birds and children sickness free during the autumn and winter with their vitamin rich seeds. When the birds come visit then they enrich the soil with their droppings for next year. I feel blessed to be cared for so generously by My Creator. I am in awe of your design and grateful for your wisdom in designing such a complex and prolific range of ecosystems that we are meant to thrive in. May we love Your Creation and treat it with the respect You intended. May the ground and ecosystem be blessed by our actions for we know that You promise that we reap what we sow. May we sow love not hate, patience not pesticides, wisdom not convenience, peace not just prosperity. May we appreciate His love gifts to us. "For God so loved the world, that he gave his only begotten Son, that whosoever believeth in him should not perish, but have everlasting life." John 3:16

Jesus, I answer your call. I want more of You Jesus. More of You in my life and soul. More of the fruits of the Spirit. More of the gifts of the Spirit. More of the Power of God in my life. No more playing Christian and no more trying to be a Christian. I want to be like You and near You and see You. No turning back, no holding back, no sitting back. All for You Jesus! I have taken a drink of the living waters and can't be satisfied with the world's feeble attempts at reaching satisfaction. I am satisfied with being Your beloved child. I look forward to forever being with You Abba Father. In Jesus Name and in the Power of Jesus Blood Amen Amen

Though I often wander
Lovingly you draw me near.
If I cry discouraged
You remove my tear.

Soon to have no tears
Soon to have no fears
When I cry Hallelujah!
In heaven Jesus hears

"And God saw everything that He had made, and, behold, it was very good. And the evening the morning were the sixth day." Genesis 1:31

"For he (God) hath made him (Jesus) to be sin for us, who knew no sin; that we might be made the righteousness of God in him (Jesus)." II Corinthians 5:21

All powerful Trinity, You uttered for the only time "very good." "Very" means true, real, and actual. True, real, actual goodness is not something we as humans have ever witnessed in full. For us there is the mark of sin and a cloud of darkness until that coming and glorious day when You will reign again. For now we see a dead leaf, or a chromosome missing, a school shooting or an ecosystem like the rainforest being destroyed, a cancerous tumor and a rusty hole in a boat. The effects of sin are far reaching and we all long for that day of rest we were created for on that sixth day. So You made another way, another path. "For as by one man's disobedience many were made sinners, so by the obedience of one shall many be made righteous." Romans 5:19 Jesus' sinless blood cleanses us from all sin and essentially its effects. God, You modeled it in our physical bodies. Blood flowing over a wound cleanses it and starts the healing process. Jesus has healed our

mortal wound of death if we will let Him. Lord, you even wrote us a health book in Leviticus called the Law so that we wouldn't have to have the extreme consequences of sin here in this world too. The sixth commandment states thou shalt not commit adultery. As the Great Physician You knew our hearts and knew that extramarital and homosexual sex brings consequences such as damage to self esteem[24],trust in others[24] AIDS[26], STD's[25], attachment disorders[25], abortion[25], ...the list goes on. You wanted to keep us from more pain. You want our life to be very good. Thank you! You want us to be righteous and free from the baggage of sin's consequences. You desire for us to soar, and be healed in Jesus' Name. Lord, teach us more of You and grant Your Spirit to be upon our lives and the lives of our loved ones as we pursue Your Righteousness. Love and respect, AK

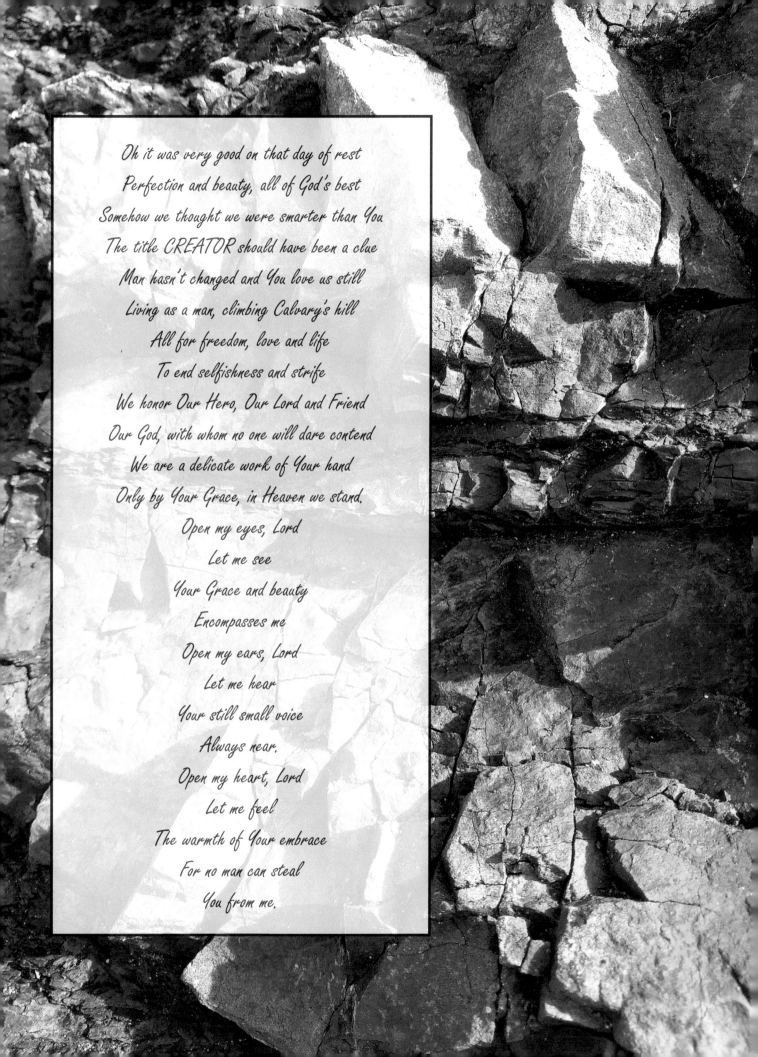

Oh it was very good on that day of rest

Perfection and beauty, all of God's best

Somehow we thought we were smarter than You

The title CREATOR should have been a clue

Man hasn't changed and You love us still

Living as a man, climbing Calvary's hill

All for freedom, love and life

To end selfishness and strife

We honor Our Hero, Our Lord and Friend

Our God, with whom no one will dare contend

We are a delicate work of Your hand

Only by Your Grace, in Heaven we stand.

Open my eyes, Lord

Let me see

Your Grace and beauty

Encompasses me

Open my ears, Lord

Let me hear

Your still small voice

Always near.

Open my heart, Lord

Let me feel

The warmth of Your embrace

For no man can steal

You from me.

A plea

Will you reader let Jesus come into your heart and cleanse it and heal it and make it new? Will you choose life and not death? Please pray this prayer with me.

Lord Jesus Christ,

I am a sinner full of sin's filthy baggage. It is weighing me down like a stage four cancer patient. I am sorry for disobeying You, and I repent of all my rebellion against You and Your wonderful plan for my life. Please heal my body, my soul so I can dedicate my all to You. Please use my past as a springboard to feed Your sheep however You choose. This is my prayer. I believe in You and grant You the proper hierarchy in my life. My God, My Father, The Great I Am! In Jesus' Name and in the Power of Jesus Blood, Amen

With love and respect,

_____(your signature)

O Lord, We adore Thee
O Lord, we adore Thee,
For Thou art the slain One
That livest forever,
Enthroned in heaven;
O Lord! We adore Thee,
For Thou hast redeemed us;
Our title to glory
We read in Thy blood.

O God, we acknowledge
Thy greatness, Thy glory!
For of Thee are all things
On earth and in heaven;
How rich is Thy mercy!
How great Thy salvation!
We bless Thee, we praise Thee:
Amen, and Amen.

(lyric by Mary Bowley) [18]

References:

1. www.genome.gov
2. m.space.com
3. www.hymnary.org
4. www.nasa.gov
5. water.usgs.gov
6. www.allaboutbirds.org
7. Animals.nationalgeographic.com
8. Sea Turtles- A Complete Guide to Their Biology, Behavior, and Conservation. James Spotila, 2004
9. a-z-animals.com
10. scienceline.ucsb.edu
11. www.nps.gov
12. www.sharefaith.com
13. www.planetnatural.com
14. www.monsanto.com
15. www.guttmacher.org Trends in Abortion in the United States 1973-2011 pdf, Jan 2014
16. umm.edu
17. Mountain Breezes: The collected poems of Amy Carmichael. Fort Washington, Pennsylvania: Christian Literature Crusade, 1999.
18. A few Hymns and some Spirtual Songs selected 1856 for The Little Flock. Addison, IL: Bible Truth Publishers, 1881.
19. Francesco Bianchini and Francesco Corbetta. Health Plants of the World, Atlas of Medicinal Plants. New York. Newsweek Books. 1977
20. www.songlyrics.com
21. songsofpraise.org
22. www.psalty.com
23. Cyberhymnal.org
24. Divorcesupport.about.com
25. www.heritage.org Robert Rector, Kirk Johnson, Shannan Martin, and Lauren Noyes. Harmful Effects of Early Sexual Activity and Multiple Sexual Partners Among Women: A Book of Charts. June 2003
26. Healthland.time.com Alice Park. HIV continues to Spread Among Gay Men, Studies Show 2012

Printed in the United States
by Baker & Taylor Publisher Services